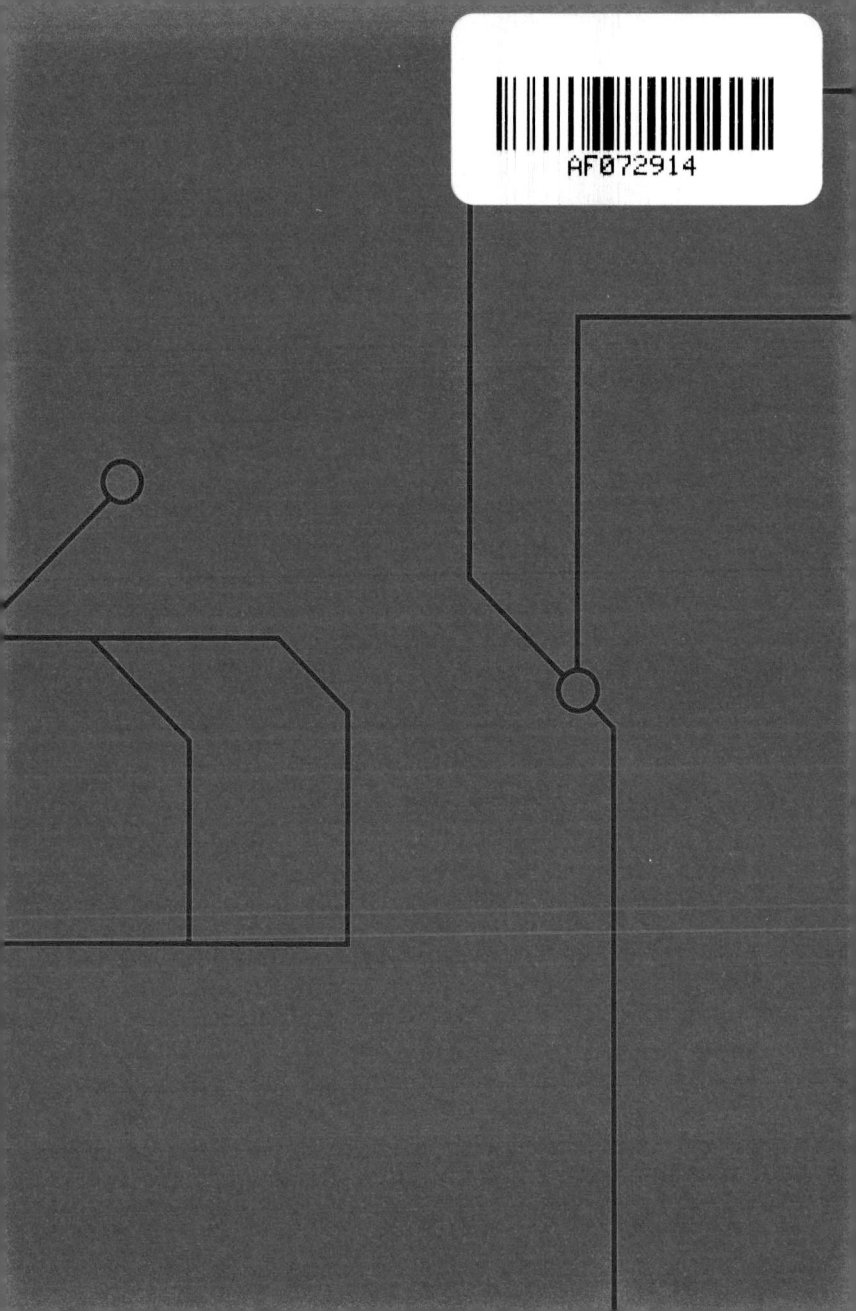

THE SLIME-ORIFIC, GHOSTLY, GHASTLY, DOWNRIGHT SPOOKY, STAY-ON-THE-ISLAND (IF YOU DARE) GUIDE TO NEW YORK CITY

VAN SIAS

RUNNING PRESS
PHILADELPHIA

TM & © 2024 Columbia Pictures Industries, Inc. All Rights Reserved.

Hachette Book Group supports the right to free expression and the value of copyright. The purpose of copyright is to encourage writers and artists to produce the creative works that enrich our culture.

The scanning, uploading, and distribution of this book without permission is a theft of the author's intellectual property. If you would like permission to use material from the book (other than for review purposes), please contact permissions@hbgusa.com. Thank you for your support of the author's rights.

Running Press
Hachette Book Group
1290 Avenue of the Americas, New York, NY 10104
www.runningpress.com
@Running_Press

First Edition: September 2024

Published by Running Press, an imprint of Hachette Book Group, Inc.
The Running Press name and logo are trademarks of Hachette Book Group, Inc.

The Hachette Speakers Bureau provides a wide range of authors for speaking events. To find out more, go to www.hachettespeakersbureau.com or email HachetteSpeakers@hbgusa.com.

Running Press books may be purchased in bulk for business, educational, or promotional use. For more information, please contact your local bookseller or the Hachette Book Group Special Markets Department at Special.Markets@hbgusa.com.

The publisher is not responsible for websites (or their content) that are not owned by the publisher.

Print book cover and interior design by Tanvi Baghele.

ISBN: 978-0-7624-8687-8

Printed in China

LREX

10 9 8 7 6 5 4 3 2 1

FRIGHT THIS WAY ...

07 *INTRODUCTION*

08 COLUMBUS CIRCLE

10 COURTHOUSE ON 40 CENTRE STREET

12 550 CENTRAL PARK WEST

16 FIREHOUSE—GHOSTBUSTERS HQ

21 GRACIE MANSION

22 MANHATTAN MUSEUM OF ART

26 THE NEW YORK PNEUMATIC RAILROAD

29 NEW YORK PUBLIC LIBRARY, MAIN BRANCH

32 PIER 34

34 RAY'S OCCULT BOOKS

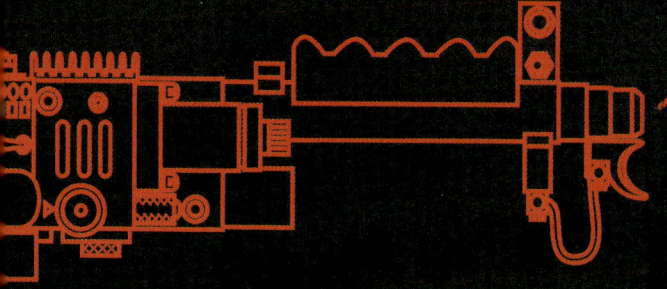

- **36** RIVERSIDE RUN
- **37** THE SEDGEWICK HOTEL
- **38** STATUE OF LIBERTY
- **40** 325 E. 77TH STREET AND FIRST AVENUE
- **42** TIMES SQUARE
- **44** YELLOW TAXICABS

INTRODUCTION

There's so much to see and do in the Big Apple, even for the most jaded New Yorker.

For those who think they've done it all, there could be something strange in your neighborhood that's worth a deeper look. Here's a guide to some haunted spots around the city to visit as well as some tips on things to do that you might not have known could go from normal to paranormal, ordinary to extraordinary—or just downright scary. Visit these places at your own risk. (We need to say that for legal reasons.)

Anyway, check these spooky spots out, you city-dwelling adventurer, you.

COLUMBUS CIRCLE

Walking through New York City, one can expect to experience some unusual sights—no matter how long you've been here. And vision isn't the only sense that can be affronted: remember that maple syrup smell that wafted over Manhattan a while back? The one that had everyone craving pancakes? It's gone, but if you're looking for a pleasant—and tummy-rumbling—scent still lingering in the air, Columbus Circle is the place to visit. Several decades ago a gargantuan Stay Puft Marshmallow Man appeared near the famous Christopher Columbus monument and stomped down Central Park West. His rampage was stopped, and although the sticky mess is now cleaned up, the smell of s'mores lingers, inspiring many a camping trip over the years.

COURTHOUSE ON 40 CENTRE STREET

Manhattan's courthouses, some of which have been around since nearly the birth of the city, are known as institutions where the law of the land is upheld and verdicts are handed

down. Protests against some of those rulings have taken a turn toward the metaphysical in the past, like back in the late 1980s, when the dastardly Scoleri brothers—who met their fate by way of electric chair—shared their dissatisfaction, using some exotic slime to help make their voices heard. They were eventually trapped, but not before leaving the room in shambles and making a complete mockery of the phrase "order in the court."

550 CENTRAL PARK WEST

There are few, if any, pieces of real estate more enviable than a spot along the most popular public park in the world. And 550 Central Park West—with its stunning views and proximity to the park—is no exception. Doorman service, dozens of spacious units, and modern appliances are some of the standout features of this apartment building. Granted, the appliances might be a little *too* modern. A refrigerator in one of the upper units has been reported to serve as a gateway to the temple of Gozer, an evil god intent on destroying the world.

All of that might have to do with the construction of the apartment building: the architect, Ivo Shandor, used cold-riveted girders with a selenium core, while the roof cap is made from a material NASA would later use for its galaxy-exploring endeavors. Back in 1920, after the First World War, Shandor thought humanity was too sick to survive, so he started a cult of Gozer worshippers who would perform rituals to bring about worldwide destruction. The building is essentially designed to attract and harness evil spiritual energy.

But those views can't be beat!

FIREHOUSE— GHOSTBUSTERS HQ

It's amazing what a little—well, actually, a lot—of elbow grease can accomplish. Once there was a dilapidated firehouse that no one in their right minds would consider buying due to its structural integrity—or lack thereof. But in the 1980s it was transformed to house an elite fighting unit.

Although it did feature a kitchen, office space, and sleeping quarters, the place still appeared as if it could crumble down at any moment due to metal fatigue on the load-bearing parts. Or it might possibly go up in a blaze due to its faulty wiring—which would be somewhat ironic for a firehouse. The fact that it had a pole that enabled one to slide from the top floor to the bottom was perhaps its saving grace, leading to its eventual purchase and renovation by the Ghostbusters.

Once it was up and running, the place became an office, laboratory, garage, storage unit, and more—similar to its original incarnation, with the occupants basically on-site between emergencies. When the group returned from their missions, they'd store the busted ghosts in a high-voltage laser containment system in the basement, proving once again that the place had potential.

That spirit prison was practically impregnable. But, as it turns out, one thing could crack it: bureaucracy. The city's Environmental Protection Agency had its sights set on the ghost-busting operation from the start. After obtaining a warrant to put the place under stricter regulations, the EPA had the power shut down on the containment system, creating a level of chaos never seen before. All the ghosts escaped and wreaked havoc across the island. Months of hard work was undone, but eventually things were returned to normal. The headquarters was shut down for a spell, due to the aftereffects of that fateful night, but it opened back up for business after the next disaster.

GRACIE MANSION

After a long day of being the leader of the biggest city in the world, the New York City mayor needs a place to hang his hat, and for close to a century, that place has been Gracie Mansion, one of the city's oldest wooden structures. Not everyone chooses to call it home while they serve, but for those who do, the mansion can be very accommodating. Located on the Upper East Side, parts of the historic landmark are open for visitors—even some unwelcome ones. Despite his status as one of the first tenants, former Mayor Fiorello La Guardia once made an unexpected pop-in—decades after being "out of the office." He might know a lot about the mansion, but you probably wouldn't want a tour guide who hasn't been alive for over forty years.

MANHATTAN MUSEUM OF ART

This cultural institution has brought new life to its pieces through the painstaking and detail-obsessed efforts of its restoration department.

And perhaps they've gone a tad overboard in the past with some of their efforts. When the museum set out to restore a life-size portrait of Vigo—the Scourge of Carpathia, the Sorrow of Moldavia—for an exhibit, the sense of foreboding was said to be near instantaneous. Some in the department stated they felt as though Vigo's eyes were following them. Those suspicions were just the tip of the iceberg, as the evil tyrant tried to devise a way to return to the mortal realm and enslave the world. To come back, he needed to take possession of a child to break his interdimensional exile.

And that was only part of his diabolical plan.

Drawing on the emotional energy generated by psycho-kinetic slime, Vigo was able to escape his banishment and fully launch his scheme. As he got closer to his ultimate goal, the sorcerer encased the museum in a seemingly unbreakable slime shell that was able to withstand proton energy blasts.

was done and all returned to normal. The museum remains a cultural touchstone in the city, but if you visit, it would be wise to exercise caution around large-scale portraiture.

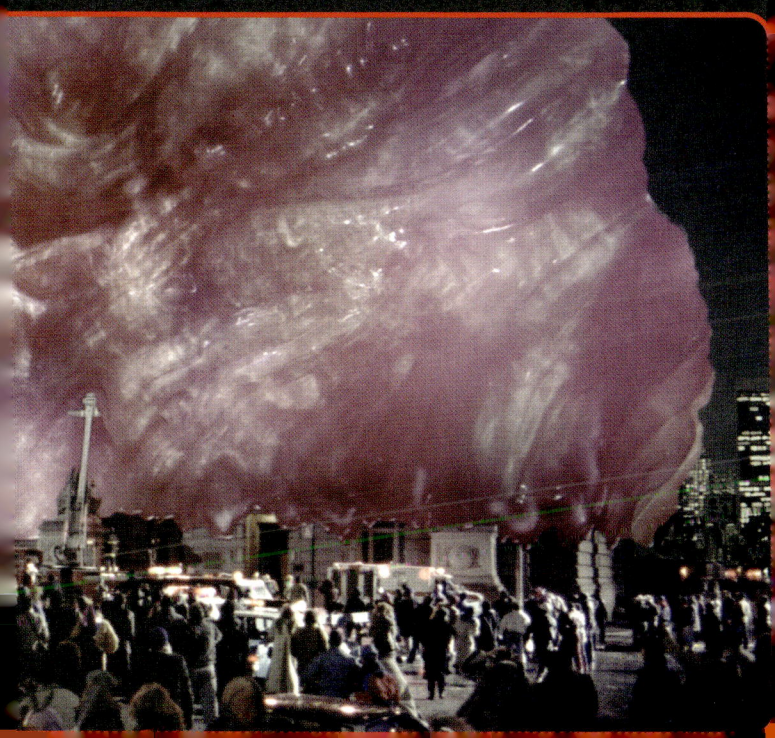

THE NEW YORK PNEUMATIC RAILROAD

While it seems like Manhattanites and the island's millions of visitors have been riding the subway forever—and that's not just getting from the East Village to the Upper West Side—there was actually a precursor to how they travel

underground at the old Van Horne Station, which propelled a car by pneumatic air pressure. You couldn't get very far—only a few hundred feet—but it was quite the sensation in the 1800s before it closed down.

Forgotten—or, rather, never known—by most New Yorkers, the abandoned tunnel was most recently the hotspot for the evil plans laid by Vigo, the previously mentioned Scourge of Carpathia (see page 23). The abandoned tunnel proved to be the near-perfect hiding place for a river of psycho-reactive slime, which could harness the feelings of the people around it, so Vigo could use the energy for nefarious means. With no one exploring the site, the ooze was able to grow unchecked for decades because who would think to look for such a thing? As more unexplained phenomena began to take shape at the time, the source of the problems was traced back to this location.

The river of slime is no more, but if you're a transportation history buff—or just looking for a place to get in touch with your feelings—this site is a must-visit.

NEW YORK PUBLIC LIBRARY, MAIN BRANCH

As one of the city's most venerable institutions, the main branch of the New York Public Library stands out among midtown Manhattan's many buildings. The lion statues alone are a must-see, as they stand guard over what might be one of the world's most precious resources: knowledge.

Even though city dwellers are able to get answers to almost any question they may have and access all types of entertainment from various handheld devices, the library still holds a certain allure. The national landmark has a large reading area for anyone interested in its millions of books, amid other comfortable and historic spaces available to the public.

If you need something from the archives, it's definitely best to let the staff procure that for you. Books symmetrically stacked in the middle of the floor—something that hasn't been seen since the Philadelphia Mass Turbulence of 1947—is not a new way of organizing. Tomes flying from one shelf to the next, unexpected card catalog chaos, and ectoplasmic slime everywhere indicate something ominous. Libraries are supposed to be quiet, and if you're not, you could get away with a warning by a presence—a full-torso apparition—who's quite familiar with the building. However, one warning might be all you get.

PIER 34

Known for its breathtaking sunset views and picturesque jogging paths, Pier 34 is a place of tranquility alongside the Hudson River for Manhattanites. Foot traffic might be heavy at times, but looking out at the calming waters fosters a feeling of escaping the hustle and bustle. There aren't many boats docking at the pier, but one in particular did stand out: the original luxury liner, the *RMS Titanic*, in all its ethereal glory. It only took about seventy years or so to finally reach its destination.

RAY'S OCCULT BOOKS

Open until 7:00 p.m. on weekdays and the witching hour—that is, midnight—on the weekends, Ray's Occult Books has become a landing point for those curious about unexplained phenomena. You just need to know where to look. For instance, *The Great Book of Magical Art, Hindu Magic, and East Indian Occultism* was able to tie a recent occurrence of invisible manipulation to a similar event back in 1939.

The bookstore is teeming with volumes on the supernatural, and if they don't have what you're looking for in stock, they'll track it down: *Magical Paths to Fortune and Power* being a recent example. Located on St. Mark's Place in the famed East Village, Ray's Occult Books has been in operation since the 1980s, when Dr. Ray Stantz founded it after a court order forced the local legend out of his prior, more well-known career.

With its mix of shops, restaurants, and all-around bohemia, St. Mark's Place is like its own pocket universe in the Big Apple, and Ray's Occult Books blends right in, with a vibe that needs to be experienced firsthand.

RIVERSIDE RUN

New York City can be the best place to get those steps in—aside from the doldrums of climbing subway station stairs on your way to work. There's plenty of running alongside the river, with paths both natural and man-made. Just watch out for any ghostly joggers who missed the memo on runners' etiquette. Is it really too much to say "on your left"?

THE SEDGEWICK HOTEL

One of New York City's swankiest spots, the Sedgewick Hotel, is a great place to stay with that special someone for an at-home vacation in the Big Apple or a venue for something as seemingly mundane as a business conference. With numerous rooms, a large banquet hall, and an attentive staff at the ready, the Sedgewick Hotel maintains its status as a luxury destination for New Yorkers and visitors alike.

It can be hard to get a room there, which is somewhat understandable given that an unwanted guest occupies the entire twelfth floor and runs rampant across the space.

It's been rumored that the staff knows about those bumps in the night, the food gone missing from carts outside of rooms, and spottings of ectoplasmic slime. However, the owners have instructed them to exercise discretion for their guests' sake. So, if you're looking to book a stay—and feeling a little brave—there's always the twelfth floor.

STATUE OF LIBERTY

Recognized as a beacon of freedom, the Statue of Liberty has stood tall on Ellis Island for more than a century. Taking one of the many mini-cruise options—or even a trip on the Staten Island Ferry—can get you close to one of the nation's most prominent landmarks.

However, if you can't make it to her, there's the rare chance Lady Liberty could come to you.

The Statue of Liberty has been known to be receptive to psychokinetic slime applied to its interior. And if that slime is then charged up with emotional energy, the result is the biggest oxymoron imaginable: a moving statue.

After hosting the huddled masses for decades, it makes sense that the Statue of Liberty would yearn to breathe free as well.

325 E. 77TH STREET AND FIRST AVENUE

After the occurrences at 550 Central Park West in the 1980s—you know, when statues came to life and one unit was the site of an interdimensional portal—there wasn't exactly an urge to remain a tenant. Manhattan real estate has been and always will be hot, with people clamoring for a spot in the city that never sleeps. This building has all of the trappings a New Yorker would look for in a high-rise

apartment and is located in a prime neighborhood. If you'd like a taste of the neighborhood, it might be possible to find someone renting their place out for a spell. One of the buildings has had problems with plumbing in the past, though, with psychokinetic slime gushing out of the bathtub, but other than that . . .

TIMES SQUARE

Usually, if one's seeking entertainment on Broadway in Times Square, odds are they want to go to a live performance, like a star-studded musical or a Pulitzer Prize-winning play. If your tastes lean more toward catching a picture on the big screen, there are still a few movie theaters in the area.

Sadly, one of the more distinctive cinemas in that neighborhood, Movieland, isn't around anymore. It only showed one film at a time—the complete opposite of the modern multiplex. Selections would range from big hits to cult favorites, like *Cannibal Girls*, which screened there in the late 1980s. However, things got a little too real during that fateful showing, with a ghost *actually* coming out of the screen. That didn't do much to boost future box-office receipts.

YELLOW TAXICABS

Driving through the city can be a harrowing experience—that's why it's best to leave it to the professionals. And there are the yellow cabs, which can be hailed from pretty much any corner—even with the proliferation of car-service apps.

Fair warning, though: you do need to pay a little attention to who's behind the wheel.

If you're in a hurry to get to the Columbia building, don't just jump in the first cab you see. Pay attention to your driver: if they look like they have a skin condition that can best be described as "decaying," you could be in for the ride of your life—however long that may end up being.

Similarly, ectoplasmic blobs have been known to commandeer buses on occasion. And even though it might have been for a worthy cause, like getting someone somewhere to deal with a problem bigger than a ghost-driven bus, being in a bus taken over by an ectoplasmic blob can nonetheless be somewhat jarring. If you happen to experience that, you're well within your rights to ask for a transfer.

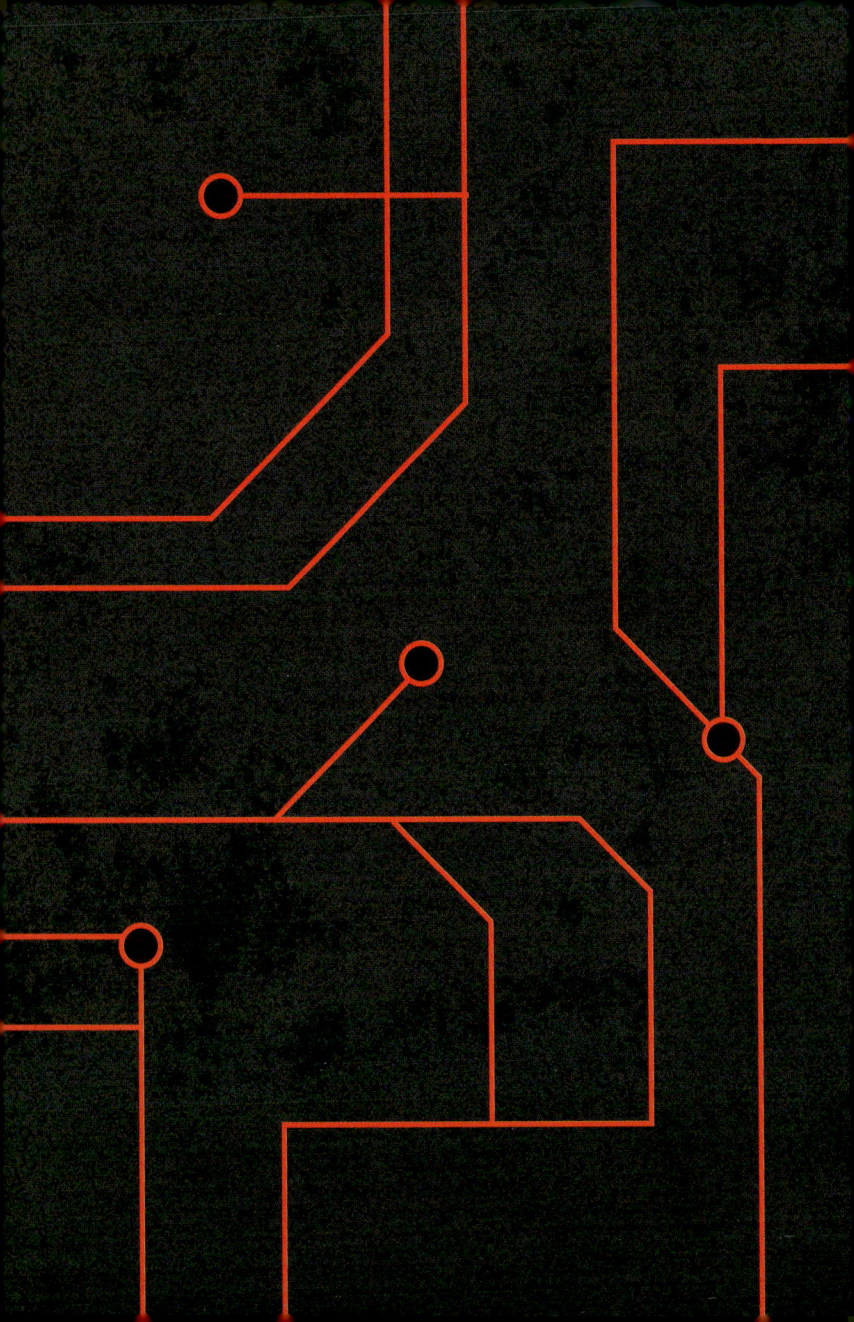

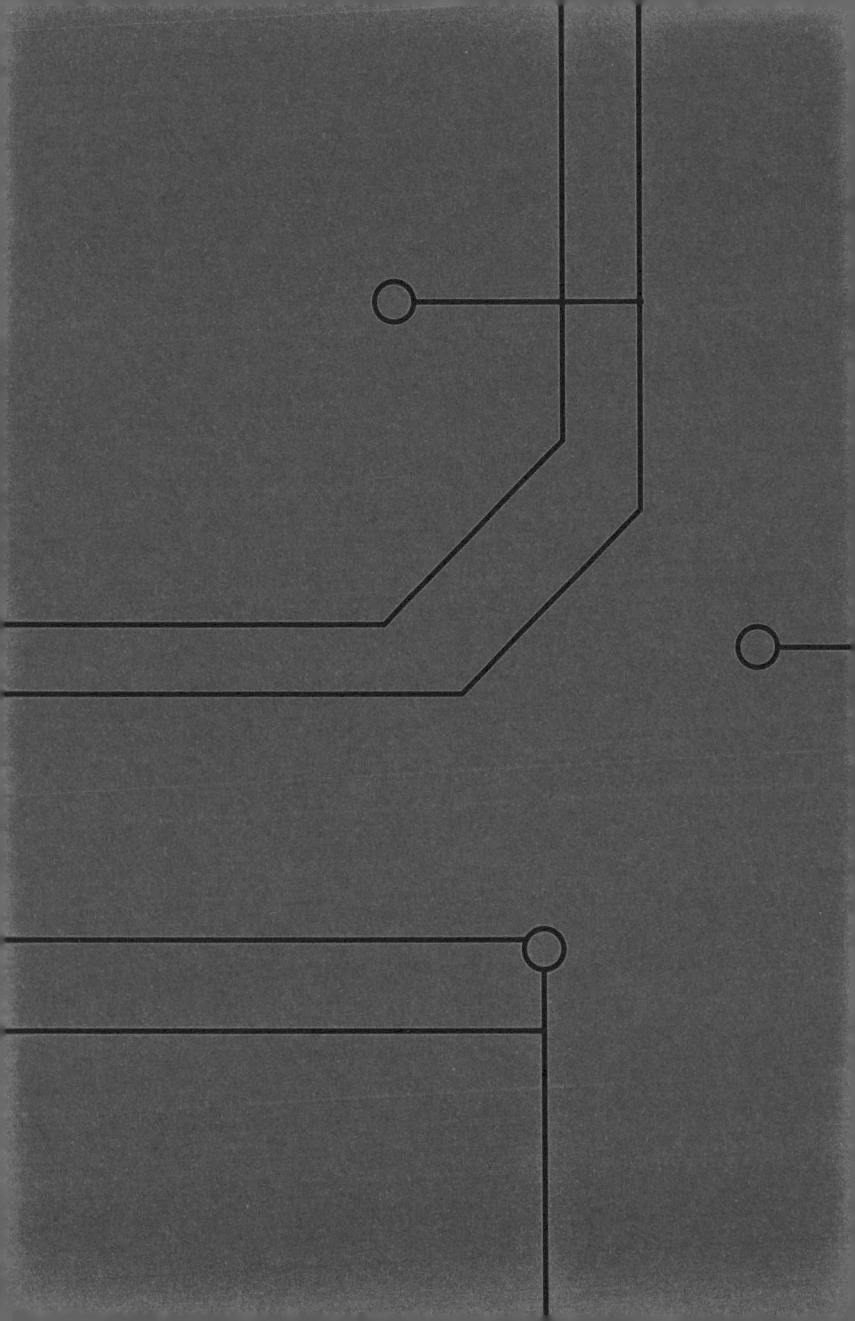